COPYWRITING LIKE THE PROS

2 In 1 Bundle

Why Copywriting Pays 6 Figures

10 Things to Make You an Epic Copy Writer

Table of Contents

WHY COPYWRITING PAYS 6 FIGURES 1
    INTRODUCTION 3
    CHAPTER 1 THE BASICS OF COPYWRITING 5
    CHAPTER 2 IT IS HARD TO SELL 13
    CHAPTER 3 LOTS OF DIFFERENT MEDIUMS... 17
    CHAPTER 4 EASY TO TAKE ON MORE PROJECTS 25
    CHAPTER 5 CLIENTS WANT PROVEN RESULTS 29
    CONCLUSION... 33

10 THINGS TO MAKE YOU AN EPIC COPY WRITER 35
    INTRODUCTION 37
    PERFORM ALL THE RESEARCH 39
    INTERVIEW THE EXPERTS 43
    HAVE YOUR OWN PERSONAL VOICE 47
    KEEP THE COPY PLAIN AND SIMPLE 49
    BE PERSISTENT 53
    FIGURE OUT YOUR OWN NICHE 55
    LOOK FOR THE HIGH QUALITY CLIENTS 57
    LEARN HOW TO WORK WITH DIFFERENT MEDIUMS 61
    CREATE A PORTFOLIO 67
    TRY SOMETHING NEW AND SEE WHERE IT LEADS 71
    CONCLUSION... 75

BOOK 1

Why Copywriting Pays 6 Figures

Introduction

Have you ever wanted to get into copywriting but are worried that it is going to take too much time to get started or that you are not going to be able to make enough money to make all of this worth your time? Do you dream about leaving your regular desk job but are worried about how you are going to pay the bills and get things done until the income starts to come to you? This guidebook is going to take some time to talk about copywriting and why this is one career choice that is going to help you to make six figures.

Copywriting is one of the most profitable careers to go into because there are so many companies that want to sell their products to the potential customers, but there are only a few copywriters who are really good at their job and can produce results. If you are able to work within deadlines, come up with copy that will stick out from all the rest, and really produce results, this is the career choice for you.

This guidebook is going to talk in more details about copywriting including why it is such a rewarding career choice for many and how you will be able to earn six figures a year with this field if you are good at the copywriting work that you do. We will take a look at some of the different things that you are able to do when it comes to picking out clients, picking out the amount of work that you want to put in and even how moving out of a niche and into a full service copywriting option will help to increase your options as well as your pay. We also look at some of the different types of clients and why it is best to go with the ones who are willing to pay you a full rate for your work.

If you are ready to get started with copywriting and want to make this your new career choice, make sure to check out this guidebook to learn how this can be such a rewarding and profitable career field for the successful copywriter to get into.

CHAPTER 1

The Basics Of Copywriting

Copywriting is a great field to get into. You will be able to work with a wide range of products and there are even many different kinds of mediums that you are able to work with. You can choose some of your favorites and see how that goes or you can choose to work as a full service option in order to offer things that are in different mediums to help the client out. Both of these are going to have advantages because sometimes a client just wants to increase their presence in one area while other times they want to start out a whole new campaign in order to reach as many customers as possible.

As you can see, there are a lot of great things that you are able to do when it comes to copywriting, but what is copywriting exactly? Copywriting is basically using writing, in its various forms, in order to sell a product to a potential customer. Sometimes the client is going to do some of the copywriting on their own, something that can be an advantage if they have the time since they know the benefits of the product better than everyone else. But most of the time the client is going to hire out a freelance copywriter (or sometimes an in house one), to do the work for them.

There are a lot of benefits that come with hiring out a copywriter. This person usually has a way with words that will help to convince the potential customer that they really need the product. They will have some time to look up research on the best customers to promote to, can work on a variety of mediums, and even try out the product with fresh new eyes to take a look at how the product really works and will benefit the customer.

You will find that there are a lot of mediums that the copywriter is able to work out of and many times they are going to work with the client on a few of them at a time. You will be able to use billboards, magazine and newspaper space, eBooks, radio and television advertisement, signs, back of park benches, blogging, and so much more. All of these are going to reach the customers that you want in different ways and it is the job of a copywriter to learn where the audience is and how to use each of these mediums properly in order to not only reach the audience, but to spur them into action.

There are a lot of hats that the copywriter is going to have to wear in order to see success. You will need to learn about the customer, learn about the product, and combine all of this together in order to create a comprehensive campaign to help out your clients. This is a lot of work in order to be successful and this is part of why the copywriter is able to bring in six figures simply by working with a few clients, and sometimes with just one client if the project is big enough, throughout the year.

At this point, you may be curious as to how you are going to be able to bring your writing to play in order to make a successful campaign for your client. You will need to bring together a lot of different things to make this happen. Some of the things that you will need in order to get started on your copywriting career and to produce some great copy for your client include:

- Exploit the benefits—the customer does not care why you think the product is amazing, they care about how the product is going to benefit them. You need to be able to explain how they are going to be able to improve their lives when they choose this product and how they should have that product right now. The more benefits you can show for the product that relate to the target audience, the easier it is to sell that product. Take the time to try out the product a few times and maybe find a few others to try out the product if you can so that you get an idea of everything that the product does and how different people will react to using the product. You can then put some of that information into your copy.

- Exploit competition's weaknesses—no matter what product you are selling, you are going to have some competition. Even as a new product, you will have some indirect competition, such as other options that the buyer can purchase besides yours, that you will have to compete with. In addition to telling the customer all the benefits of using your product, you will need to tell them what they are missing when they choose another product.

- Know the audience—you need to have a good idea of your audience. Do you think teenage girls are going to react to the same message that middle aged or elderly men do? Of course not! When you know your audience better, you can create a message that really speaks to them and you will be more persuasive to helping them to make the sale. This will require a bit of research, but make sure that you learn all about the target audiences demographics before continuing.

- Tell a story—the customer wants to hear a story and find out how the product is going to benefit them. If you just list out the facts, you are going to bore the customer in just a few minutes. Learn how the product works, figure out who may be using this product, and more, and you will be able to turn your copy into a story that sells.

- Understand the medium—there are a variety of mediums that you will be able to use in your work. You can work in print, television, radio, online, social media, blogging, and more. You can choose to work on a variety of these and offer a packaged deal to the customer, or you can just pick one or two as your niche. No matter how you go through with this, you need to make sure you understand how the medium works. Each one will need different considerations from how many words to use to the type of audience that will use them. Learn how each of the different types of media work and how you should write copy for it and you are ready to go.

- Don't forget the call to action—no matter which medium you are using, you need to have some call to action. This can be as simple as telling the customer to go purchase the product, giving them a phone number to call or even a website. The call to action will change with each product, but make sure that the customers know what they should do after reading your copy.

- Proofread—any time that you are working on a new project, make sure that you go and proofread it. You don't want to send out information to the customers that has a lot of spelling mistakes, too many words, or goes against one of the other rules of grammar that we have discussed. If you are not the best editor, find someone who can do some proofreading for you to save time, and some embarrassment for the client.

Getting into copywriting can be a rewarding career that can actually make you a pretty good income, especially if you work in freelance and choose to do this with a variety of different customers. The reason it can pay so well is that many clients are looking for good customers and want to be able to sell their products and make more money, but there are a limited amount of good copywriters out there who can do the work. If you already enjoy doing this kind of work and don't mind putting in the research and time, you have a valuable talent that a lot of businesses and clients will pay good money for.

CHAPTER 2

It Is Hard To Sell

One of the reasons that you are going to be able to make so much when you work in copywriting is that it is really hard to sell to the customers. There are thousands of businesses plus other people on social media and elsewhere who are trying to sell a product or a service to their friends and family or to other customers. This creates a lot of noise all around the customer and that can make it hard for businesses to get their name out there and to stand out from the crowd and the noise.

Because of all this noise, the customer is becoming immune to some of the advertisements that they see. This is pretty simple to understand considering that there is advertising all around them. Advertising and copywriting is going to show up in the shows that they watch (both in the commercials that come up as well as some product placement within the show), the radio shows that they like, the signs on the street and highway as they drive, the park benches when they drive, the magazines and news papers that they read, their favorite blogs and websites have copywriting, and even their social media accounts have people selling products all the time.

If the customer paid attention to this constant barrage of information and copywriting, it would not take long before they were overloaded and couldn't handle all that information. There is just so much that is going on around them that the customer is going to learn how to ignore it in the hopes of being able to get other things done throughout the day.

While this may be able to help the customer to get through the day without having too much information thrown at them, it is going to make it really hard for a copywriter to get through the noise and the fact that the customer is not going to see or listen to most of the advertising that is coming their way. This means that you are going to have to be really creative, coming up with a great copywriting that can help the client get their message across and really make some good money.

This is one of the reasons that a copywriter is going to be able to make a lot of money when they get into this field; if they are good at copywriting. The good copywriters are able to get out there and create a message that is easy to read, fits with the product that they are selling, and can actually bring in a lot of customers without more work on the part of the client. They can change the copy to a variety of different mediums and can even change up the campaign to make something new and unique on occasion when needed.

For most businesses though, it is hard to find a copywriter that is any good. There are a lot of people who have the basis and understanding of working in this field, but they don't have the experience and their copy may not be all that great. This can result in some bad copy that easily gets lost in the noise, or can even lose out because it puts the company in a bad light. Finding a good copywriter is hard to do and many clients are willing to pay some good money to find one that can produce results and will work with them for the long term.

This means that if you are able to produce some good copy that will get through to the customer in an efficient and effective way without wasting the time and money of your client, you are in for making a good income. Many of the good clients have gone the route of choosing a cheaper freelancer who does copywriting and they realize that this is not giving them the results that they want or that they just wasted money. They have decided that it is worth it to spend a bit more money in the process in order to really get someone who knows the industry, how to work with the different mediums, and who will be able to give them the results that they want.

If you are able to fit all of these requirements, which a good copywriter is going to be able to do, you will be able to work with some fantastic clients with a variety of different products and make a good paycheck doing the things that you love.

CHAPTER 3

Lots Of Different Mediums

Another reason that copywriters can make six figures is because there are so many different mediums that they are able to work on. Even if the client knows how to work on one or two of the media, there are so many others that they may want to utilize within their work and they will need to find someone who is able to handle all of them, rather than hiring one person for each of the niches. If you are able to handle the majority of these media for the client, you are going to be paid well, especially if you are efficient and can produce results. Some of the media that you may need to work with for your client in copywriting include:

Television

Television is a bit trickier than some of the other options. While it does give a big reach, it also costs a lot so you and the client will need to determine if the costs are worth it. If you are working with a client that has a national presence, this can be a good cost to incur. On the other hand, most local clients or regional ones will find that this is a waste of money and that they could be more effective in reaching their customers through some of the other media that you can choose.

Television can be a great way to reach your audience if the audience is a large group. There is a lot that you are able to do with the combination of words, pictures, and so much more. You still need to remember that there are a lot of different commercials that are on the variety of channels that you can choose from so you copy needs to be really compelling, unique, and will really help the customer to pick your product over all the other noise that is around.

Radio

Radio is one of the traditional forms of advertising and you are going to be able to do a lot of cool things with this. Remember that with this kind of advertising, you will need to use the words, as well as some sounds, to tell the story since there isn't going to be the option for using any pictures. This requires some creative energy to come up with a story and a script that will help to entice the customer, usually while they are driving, to remember about the company and the product when they get closer to a computer or the store. If you like to tell stories and your audience spends a lot of time inside of a car for a commute, you may want to consider using radio.

Newspaper

The idea of using newspaper copy outside of using it for press releases has gone out of style a bit with copywriting. Not as many people are using this method compared to who did it in the past, making it harder to find the right target audience. And depending on the audience you want to work with, you may find that your target doesn't even read the newspaper at all.

That being said, there are still a few times when you will want to use this kind of advertising. First, there are people who still read the paper, such as business people, the elderly, and so on. So you may find that putting some copy in the paper will go straight to the right people. When working in newsprint, remember that the quality of paper is low and you will most likely be stuck in black and white. Your space will be limited so be careful with how many words and pictures you try to fit into that little area.

Another option that comes with newspaper is going online. Most newspapers have moved online and will take website advertising (which can be done on blogs, social media, and pretty much any website that you would like), to promote your business. These often do have some color, but you will still be limited on the amount of space that you are able to use so keep the message short and to the point.

Magazine

Magazines can be a lot of fun to work with. These are usually a bit higher quality compared to what you are going to see with newspaper because the pages are nicer and the magazine will allow color and other images a bit better. When going with magazine copy, you want to make sure to keep it straight to the point and allow the pictures to do some of the talking. These do need to be high quality because the magazine wants to make sure that they are working with companies that produce things that stay up with their high standards.

In addition, magazines have a longer shelf life, meaning that people can come back to the advertisement and often don't just throw the magazine away at the end of the day. This gives you more chances to reach that same customer, as well as others in the home or nearby who may look at the magazine, compared to what you will get with newspaper.

Billboard

Billboard advertising is not always the most popular option for clients, but it is still a good one to offer for a few of them that may still want to go this route. Billboards can include any of the signs that are on the side of the road and that your potential customer would see while driving by. Since the customer is only going to get a short amount of time to see the copy, you need to make sure to keep it short and sweet. Most experts agree that the average time a customer gets to read your copy will be about seven seconds on the highway to make sure that you keep the copy and the slogan minimal for the best results.

Blogs

It is becoming more popular that clients will want to have a big batch of blogs written for them. This helps to increase their web presence and can make it easier to bring more customers to their products. You are going to need to know how to work with SEO in order to make this work. Basically SEO helps to rank the blog articles or the website that you are working on higher in the search engine results based on the words that you use. This doesn't mean that you should stuff a hundred of the same phrases into the website and hope that you will be fine. The information needs to be helpful to the customer and provide insight and most search engines are going to check for keyword stuffing.

If you like to learn about different topics and writing articles, this can be a great place to work for. These are usually pretty easy to write, but the client will often want bulk articles that they don't have time for. For those who are able to work on high quality articles in a fast manner, this is a good medium to get into because it is easy, efficient, and can make you some good money in the process.

Social media

Social media is quickly rising as a way to write copy for the customers and get them interested in the product that you are selling. Copywriters who work in this medium need to be able to check in often. This will include answering questions, leaving comments and posts, adding pictures, commenting on other information that people bring in, keeping the information about the page up to date, adding in new inventory and so much more. This alone is a niche that a lot of copywriters will get into exclusively because managing two or three social media accounts for one client can take some time.

Before jumping into this one, you need to be careful that you are picking out the right ones. There are many social media sites that you can work with and it isn't very efficient to work on all of them. During your research of your target audience, you should be able to figure out which social media sites they are going to frequent and then you can pick out the two or three that are going to be the best for your client and their product.

eBooks

In some cases, you will find that writing eBooks will help out your clients. They may be selling a product and wish to have an eBook written that can go along with it. This is common with many kitchen appliances, such as Air Fryers and slow cookers because you can write out a recipe book that is offered as an incentive for purchasing the product. Some clients will have someone write an eBook about a certain health product before offering some of their health services along with the book. If you like to write some of the bigger pieces or like to tell a nice story, eBooks can be a great way to make some money and since these are easy to write and make good money, you will find that this is a good medium to offer.

There are a lot of different mediums that you are going to be able to work with when you are in copywriting. Many copywriters choose to work in a wide variety of these mediums because this makes it easier to make more money. You are often going to be able to charge more to offer a full service on copywriting, meaning that you offer to do most if not all of these mediums, and will get more customers with the variety, compared to just working on one or two mediums. Remember that it is your business though and any of these can bring in customers based on your talents and the amount of time you have to devote to the work.

CHAPTER 4

Easy To Take On More Projects

When you are working in a traditional job, you only get to work with one employer or client at a time. You are given the salary that you agree upon and it is hard to make more money for the amount of work that you put in. Whether you work harder or not, you are going to make the same income each time.

While this is one of the ways that many copywriters are going to choose to do their work, it is not always the best. It can provide a steady income that is reliable and can prevent you from spending a lot of time looking for new jobs. But when you are stuck with one client, it is hard to change up your rates, take on more work, or be in control of the amount of money that you are making for all your work.

The best thing about this career choice is all the freedom that you are going to be able to get from it. You can pick the amount that you want, changing some rates based on the type of project and how much work you will need to do with each one, and even taking on the amount of work that you are comfortable with. when all of this is combined, you will find that it is easier than ever to make the six figures you are looking for when working in copywriting.

CHAPTER 5

Clients Want Proven Results

When it comes to copywriting, clients want proven results. They don't want to hire someone who may have simply written a few articles in the past and then hopefully they will be able to put together a whole campaign to sell a product. They want someone who has experience, someone who has done this work and can prove that the work was successful, and these clients are willing to pay a premium to get this.

Most clients understand that they are going to get what they pay for. If they are going to spend money on this campaign and they want to make money on their product, they understand that they need to pick out a copywriter who knows what they are doing and can bring in results. The client would rather pay a little bit more to get the good results the first time rather than paying someone new to do the work, wasting time and money, and then having to pay the professional to come in and clean up the mess.

You will find that the good clients know how much you are worth. If you are working with a client that wants to pay a low rate, there are a few things that are going on here. First, the client is either not aware of the current rate for a good copywriter and is just guessing at how much they will need to pay for the work to get done. Another issue could be that they are having issues with their cash flow and they are hoping for a miracle to happen such as a good copywriting offering to do the services for a great price so they can get their business back up and running. And in other cases, the client is just trying to get work for free and they don't really care how hard you work, as long as they get the results that they want for a way below market value amount.

No matter the reason for the lower amount offered on a job, you don't want to work with any of these clients. The first client doesn't know your true value and may be difficult to work with in the long term. Now you can talk to them about the price and some will realize that they need to pay more and will be happy to do it, but others will still want to get the discounted price because that is all they want to pay and they think the work is "easy enough for anyone to do." You don't want to work for these people because they won't value you work and you will spend way too much time making very little money.

For the second group of clients, you need to be careful. There is usually a reason that they are short on cash or have cash flow issues and often this means that they are about to fail. You are not only going to miss out on some of the good income that you should be making, but the company is likely going to fail and you won't make a good income at all from them.

And finally, no one wants to work with someone who purposely puts the value too low. Many times these clients disappear and never even pay, leaving you with a lot of wasted time and no money to show for it. Even if the client does end up paying you for the work that you do, you will find that they are really difficult to work with, will request way too many changes, and you will spend more time than it is worth to get the work done.

Finding the clients who will pay the rates that you deserve is critical. This is going to help out in a number of ways. First, they are going to value your time. Perhaps these clients have worked with some bad copywriters in the past and they are willing to pay more to get the results that they want or they know the market value for what they want. Once you prove that you are the person they want to work with, you are going to be able to get those good priced jobs that are going to make your income go through the roof.

But before you can get these better prices, you need to make sure that you are able to produce those results. There are plenty of those clients that will pay the attractive rates, but they are not going to pay those rates to just anyone. You will need to have a method to show how you have been successful with these kinds of campaigns in the past. You will need to show some of the work that you have done with copywriting in the past and if you have some numbers in place to show how successful they were, you will be able to impress the clients even more.

As a good copywriter, you should be able to show that you are going to bring in the results for the client. A good client is willing to pay some of the higher rates, but you do need to make it worth their time. These clients are going to pay for the results, not just for your time to create the work. If there aren't any results, you are going to have some issues getting the income that you want.

Conclusion

Working in copywriting can be a really rewarding career choice. You get to work with writing and in so many different mediums that there is always something new that you get to work in. For people who are looking to put their selling and writing techniques to the test, especially those who want to work on a freelance basis, working in copywriting is the method to go. It is fun, provides some challenges, and as this guidebook shows, it can help you to earn six figures a year from your own home.

In this guidebook, we have taken a look at all the great things that you will be able to do in order to increase the rate that you can charge. The fact that you are able to pick out your clients, work in the medium of your choice, and even that you are able to produce some great results will make it easier to earn the money that you want.

When you are tired of going to work and making someone else rich, why not check out this guidebook and learn how you will be able to make a six figure income from copywriting.

BOOK 2

10 Things to Make You An Epic Copy Writer

When you are ready to get started with this new career change, make sure to check out this guidebook and see what the ten best things are that you can do to become an epic copywriter as soon as possible.

Perform All The Research

One of the first things that you are going to need to work on when it comes to being a copywriter is that you will need to perform all of the necessary research. How are you going to be able to sell a product to your customers if you don't know everything about the product or about the audience who would like to purchase it.

The first thing that you can do is to learn about the product. You should be able to get a lot of the information from the client about their product or services, including how it is made, how much it is for, and more. In addition to this, it is a good idea to take some time and try out the product yourself. See if the client will send you a version of the product so that you can put it to use and figure out how you will be able to sell it to others.

There are two main types of research that you will be able to do in order to get your information about the audience that you would like to use; primary and secondary. The primary research is important because it allows you to have time talking to the customers, or people who fit into the demographics of the customers you want to sell to, and you can gain valuable information from them. Since these are the people that you want to sell to in the first place, you will be able to ask them about their spending and selling habits and what would get them to purchase a product.

This is often considered one of the best ways to get information, but it does take more time so you may be a bit limited on how much information you are able to get this way. This is why secondary research can be a good option as well. This allows you to look at studies, documents, and more to get information. Someone else has gathered the information and it may not be exactly on the target audience that you want, but it can really provide you some useful information without taking up as much time.

When it comes to working in copywriting, it is often best to do some mix of the two types of research. You should spend some time getting primary research from surveys, polls, and interviews, as much as possible before you go in and look at the secondary research. You will then be able to combine these both, along with your own personal use of the product, in order to make some of the best copy possible.

Research is not something that a lot of people like to work on. Copywriters are often writers and they just want to sit down and let the words flow. But while you may be able to come up with some impressive copy by doing this, it is not necessarily going to be the right copy for the audience that you have in mind. Doing this research is going to ensure that you not only find the right audience for a particular product or service, but that you also learn the best way to advertise to this audience to get them to purchase the product.

Interview The Experts

Are you just starting to look into being a copywriter and are interested in learning more about how the process works, how to pick out good clients, where you should price yourself at for different projects and so on? One of the best ways that you are going to be able to get these questions answered is by asking some of the experts.

No matter what field you are choosing to go into, you will find that there are some experts who can help. These are people who have been in the field for some time, the people who have already done the work and who will be able to give you some advice along the way. If you are able to find an expert who is willing to help you out, make sure to utilize them as much as you can without being annoying or getting in the way.

The best kind of expert that you can work with is someone who has worked in copywriting in the past. This should be someone who has had success with this kind of work, but they can work in almost any field without copywriting including social media, agency experience, freelancing, and more. They will be able to give you some advice on where to start with looking for clients, take a look at your portfolio and tell you what will work and what is not the best idea, and so much more.

Sometimes it is hard to find an expert that is specifically in the field of copywriting. This does not mean that you are lost without someone to help. As a copywriter, you may find that you are doing a lot of your work freelance so why not ask someone who has worked in the freelance industry to help you out. There are a ton of people who are in this kind of industry, working in writing, computer work, graphic design, and more who can easily give you some of the advice that you need. It may not particularly pertain to the copywriting world, but many freelancers experience the same kinds of issues in terms of finding clients and keeping track of their finances and such and you will be able to find a lot of the information that you need along the way.

If you can't find someone to be your mentor through this process, consider sitting down with them just once and asking some questions like in an interview. Most experts are flattered to get some time to talk with you about their work and they will be willing to sit down and talk for a short while. Be prepared with some questions and consider recording these just in case you need them down the line.

Finding a good expert is one of the best things that you can do to ensure that you are getting the best advice for how to get started. Make sure that you are appreciative of their time and not bothering them too much, but asking a few questions and asking for advice on occasion is a great way to learn something new and to make yourself stand out when you want to work in the copywriting field.

Have Your Own Personal Voice

One of the best ways to stand out when you are working in copywriting is to have your own personal voice. This is shown in the way that you write things out on paper, similar to the voice and mannerisms that you have when you talk to friends and family. Some of the best copywriters are able to let this shine through without ruining the main point of the copy, helping to give a bit of personality to their writing and to what they are selling.

There are many ways that you are able to let your own personal voice come through when you are writing. You can choose to use certain words or phrases based on the things that you would normally say to others around you. You can add in certain punctuation marks or grammar rules. This may seem harder than it is, but usually when you are writing, there is a certain "tone" that comes in that is considered your voice. You simply need to learn how to use this to your advantage to make it more enjoyable for others to read the copy that you are writing.

Of course, you need to be careful with going overboard with this. You shouldn't take this as a license to make poor grammar mistakes, add in extra words that aren't needed at the end of every sentence (like darling or something similar), or have your voice take over the copy and distract form the item or service that you are trying to sell. Your voice can either make or break the copy that you are trying to sell so be careful and use it as a tool and you will find that it makes a big difference.

Overall, having your own personal voice come through your writing is one of the ways that you will be able to set your work apart from the work that someone else does. No one else is able to write in the same way that you do so make that inner voice shine and learn how to really impress your clients.

Keep The Copy Plain And Simple

Yes, during this process you are trying to sell a product to the customer, but you still need to keep the copy plain and simple. You don't want to add in too many words or write copy that is hard to understand or will be lost in the meaning when the customer is trying to read your work. Your work needs to be plain and simple for the customer to understand so that they can see the benefits and make a decision in your favor.

Think about working on a billboard. Your customers are going to see the billboard, but they are really only going to have about seven seconds at the most in order to read what is on the sign. This means that you only have room to put a few words on that really have meaning and everything else is going to be lost. A big paragraph or more of information may seem useful, but the customer will not be able to read it while driving by. You have to keep the language simple and concise, perhaps just a few words or a short sentence, so they understand your product and will want to learn more or will make the purchase.

Now, when working with other forms of copywriting, you will usually have more freedom than the billboard to write more words. These other forms are usually looked at for longer periods of time by the customer so you can write out more. But you still need to be careful with the things that you are writing on them. Adding in extra words or missing out on important concepts will make it hard for the reader to get the message that you want.

So, a good thing to do is just write out all the information that you have in your head. Don't worry about how it sounds or if it all flows together at this point, just sit down and write. Once you are done, take a step back from the work for at least an hour, though overnight is best. The next day, come back and circle or highlight the things that you want to keep and cross out the things that aren't going to work.

By now, you should at least have the start to the information that you want to use in your copywriting. You will be able to form the ideas together if they seem a bit fragmented. After time, you will have the copy saying and looking the way that you want. Now it is time to go through and cross out the words that you don't need or that are taking up the extra space. Go through and see which words you can eliminate without changing and throw them all out. You can cut down considerably on your word usage and space with this simple step while still getting the information out to the client.

Clear and concise writing is one of the best that you can do to ensure that your customers are going to get the message and actually feel like they are going to benefit from the product or service you are trying to sell. Try some of these tips for writing clear and concise copy and see what a difference it can make.

Be Persistent

Starting out as a beginner can be tough. You want to be able to get that first client and start making money, whether you are doing this as a part time gig or you want to make it full time, but landing clients at all, much less enough to help you to make money can be frustrating. Most clients want a worker who has a lot of experience or the good ones are already working with someone that they know and trust. This can make it hard for the beginner to get their foot in the door.

In addition, it is sometimes hard to get started and keep going if you have some issues with a bad client along the way. Spending all your hard earned time on a project just to have more added to the work or have the client disappear without paying can be frustrating. But overall, you need to keep going through it, and learn from your issues with the client, and you are going to come out on top.

All copywriters had to work hard to make it successful. They all had a bad client or two that made them rethink whether this is the right career choice for them and they all had trouble landing those first few clients. But the difference between the successful copywriters and the unsuccessful ones is that they never gave up. They kept looking for those good clients, they kept growing their skills, and they never gave up trying to make it happen.

As a new copywriter, there are a lot of things that can get in your way and make it hard to stick with all the work. But you need to be persistent. Keep looking for those new clients, keep looking for new ways to expand your skills and your knowledge (even if this means that you need to go and take some classes to learn something new) and even keep making connections so that you are able to find the right clients, and the right kind of work, that makes you happy.

There are going to be times when you feel down about the work or like you are never going to be able to find right answers to getting things done. But with the right attitude and the idea that you should never give up, you will find that you are able to bring in those first clients, make some good money, and actually enjoy the work that you are doing in your life!

Figure Out Your Own Niche

There are a lot of different things that you will be able to do when you go into copywriting. You can choose to work on eBooks that go along with a certain product that you are selling (something that is common with things such as kitchen appliances and tools). You can choose to work in social media and bring the company into the modern work with some of the great messages and posting that you are able to do through this. You can specialize in working on print advertisements like magazines, billboards, blogging newspapers and more. Or some people like to focus on the options like television and radio copy that helps to bring the message home in a different way.

Choosing between one or two of these niches can really help you to market yourself to different clients. You need to make sure that your portfolio has some of these items from your niche inside to ensure that neglect to pay for you and just disappear when the work is done.

As a beginner, you are going to run into more of these clients than you would probably like to admit. There are always shady clients who are going to look at you and think that they are able to take advantage of you. But there are a few things that you can do to watch out for those bad clients including:

- The price is too high—if you are looking at a job posting and notice that the price is really high for the work, higher than what is considered normal for the work that is requested, you should run away. These clients are usually just trying to attract beginners to do the work. The issue is that they will promise all this money but won't sign a contract at all and often take the work without ever offering a payment. Always be careful if the rate doesn't seem to fit in line with what is usual in the industry.

- The price is too low—most clients will list out how much they are willing to pay for the work. If you notice that the price is pretty low, it is probably not worth your time. The client will expect to get high quality work, for a price that is well below market value and you will probably waste your time. Make sure to charge a rate that you are comfortable with and stick to that.

- Won't do a contract ahead of time—it is always a good idea to get started with a new client by writing out a contract. This is going to be a good way to protect you and the client. This contract is going to list out all the things that will happen while you are working together including the work to be completed, the cost, and the deadlines. If a client won't fill out the agreement, there is probably something that is going wrong and you need to be careful.

- Clues inside the posting—sometimes you will be able to see that there are issues with the client within their posting. If the wording keeps changing, there are issues with the grammar, or something else seems off with the posting, you should proceed with caution and look for another client to work with.

- The workload changes—when you read through the job posting, you will look to see what the workload is about and then fill out your application. Sometimes though, you will spend time talking to a client and they will try and change the scope of the work or add on a lot more and still want to pay the same price. These clients often prove to be difficult to work with and will keep changing the scope or adding on more work without paying you extra. Set out the terms right away and only do the work that was agreed to.

- Client is hard to get ahold of—if you are having trouble getting your client to answer your emails or calls and the job hasn't even been awarded yet, you may need to worry. Times get busy, but if your client goes days without talking to you and then all of a sudden shows up again, you are probably dealing with a difficult client. Give them some time to respond, but if it seems to take too long, it may be best to pick someone else to work with.

Learning when to spot a bad client is one of the best things that you can do for your career. There are a ton of clients who are excellent, pay well, and are a joy to work with and you will find plenty of these along your journey. But you will find that one bad client can ruin it all for you. So make sure that you are looking for some of these signs each time that you apply for a new job and find out which clients are the best for you.

Learn How To Work With Different Mediums

When it comes to copywriting, there are a lot of different medium types that you are able to use. These help the client to reach as many of their clients as possible based on where they are located or what mediums they are more likely to use. For example, if you are going to try to talk to a demographic of teenagers, it is more likely that you would reach them through television, social media, and blogs compared to an older generation that may be more prone to reading through the newspaper and magazines.

Understanding your demographics is important if you want to be able to really reach them the right way. There are so many different options that you can choose from and unless your client has an unlimited budget, you will find that your client will not want to pay for all these mediums. In fact, even if the client has a lot of money to spend, they still will want to spend it in the proper way and only use the mediums that they need.

So first, you will need to determine the mediums that are going to speak the best to your target audience. You will be able to do this through the right research like we talked about before. Once you know your demographics and have a good idea of which mediums you would like to work with, it is time to get to work. Let's take a look at some of the different mediums that you may choose and how you will write things out differently for each one:

- Television—television copy is a big one when it comes to selling a product and it can work with both local and national companies. You will need to tell a story with this one as well, but since you are using pictures in this one, you will have the advantage over the other options. You still need to make it stand out from some of the other commercials that are on and show off the benefits of your product, but sometimes this one is a bit easier.

- Radio—when it comes to radio copywriting, you need to tell a story. You won't be able to use pictures or images to help the customer out. So you need to have really descriptive language that will tell a story and make the listener feel something. This can take some practice to do, but be careful to not use sound effects that will scare the driver or something like sirens that will make them upset when they are driving.

- Billboard—these are going to be short and sweet. Do not spend more than a short line on these. You have to remember that when people see a billboard, they are going to get seven seconds or less of reading it; they won't have time to read through a whole book. Find a good slogan or a short sentence that grabs their attention and gets the customer to check out your product.

- Blogs—sometimes it is a good idea to work on blog articles to make sure that you are reaching the customers. Many clients decide that they want to start out a blog, usually attached to their website, in order to use SEO and bring in the customers before sending them to a link of the product. You can write about many different topics that relate to the product to get the customers, but you do need to be careful about sounding too salesy in the process.

- Websites—sometimes your client is going to want you to work on their website. This is the first area of attack for a lot of companies because they have a lot of customers who will choose to check out this area ahead of time before moving on to purchasing the product. You may be responsible for keeping news up to date on the site, adding a home page, an about me page, and other pages based on what the customer needs.

- Social media—social media is a great place to start if you are working with teenagers and young adults as your target audience. This allows you to work with lots of pictures, screenshots, and more to reach the audience. There are countless options that you are able to use when it comes to social media so you will have some work deciding which ones are the best for your target audience. Keep the messages short and simple, show off the new benefits or products for the client, and answer any questions that your customers have in order to see the results.

- Print—print copy can be a lot of fun because there are so many sizes and choices that you can make. Sometimes you are writing something in a small area and have to be really concise and sometimes you are going to get a bit more space. Magazine and newspaper print ads are going to be a bit different in terms of quality as well. Either way, it is important to keep things simple with just a few sentences and a nice high quality picture that will show the audience what you are all about.

With all the different mediums that are available for you to choose from, there is a lot of variety that can make working in copywriting a lot of fun. Learn how to use each of these mediums and what can make them effective and you have a great start to selling your products or service.

Create A Portfolio

One of the biggest things that you are able to do when working on copywriting is to get started with your portfolio. Your clients are going to want the chance to see some of your work. This is basically like proof that you have experience in this work and allows the client the ability to look through your work and see if you have the right voice for what they have in mind. Without the portfolio you are going to find that it is hard to get the work that you want.

If you have done some marketing or writing work in the past, even if it doesn't relate directly to copywriting, it is a good idea to get started with using these in your portfolio. Make sure to have a lot of variety in your portfolio so that the client is able to see all that you are able to do and to get a good idea of whether or not you will be able to bring them the work that they are looking for.

On the other hand, if you are someone who is a beginner to the whole copywriting business, you may find that it is hard to put together the portfolio that you need. This doesn't mean that you should avoid sending out a portfolio at all; if you avoid sending out this portfolio in your application, you are going to find that a lot of clients will refuse to work with you since they just don't know what you are able to produce.

So what are you supposed to do when you don't have any items to add into your portfolio because your past work? It is time to put in a bit of hard work ahead of time. Pick a couple of companies that you really admire and want to work with and then use these to make some great portfolio pieces. You can choose whether you want to write out a few pieces on each of them or do a whole campaign on them like you would for one of your clients.

The more information you are able to put into your portfolio, the better you will be able to convince the client that you are the right candidate for them. If you are only working on the blog postings or the television spots, you may need to work on a few different companies to get this information. On the other hand, many people like to work on full campaigns as this brings in more money and can be easier to get jobs for (clients want to have full service agencies rather than hiring someone out for each part), so you may just need one or two companies to get this stuff into your portfolio.

When you are working on these portfolio pieces, make sure that you are taking the whole process seriously. These are pieces of work that you will show to potential clients, the work that is going to show that you are a serious copywriter. If you mess around and don't take this stuff seriously, you will find that the client will pick someone else. Pretend that you are working on a project for a client in order to make it look professional.

Over time, you will have completed a few projects for various clients, and you can add these real examples into your portfolio. These are going to be more poignant and will really show how your work goes compared to some of the other options that you may use. Make sure that you start adding these new parts to your portfolio as they come in so that you have something stronger to show your future clients.

Try Something New And See Where It Leads

If you always do the same thing that has been done in the past, you are going to be stuck doing the same, or worse, than you were before. It is always a good idea to try out something new that you think will really respond with the customers and get them to make the purchase that the client wants.

Customers like to see things that are brand new and exciting. When they look on television or read through blogs, they always see the same few advertisements come up and it gets boring. None of them are going to stick with the customer and those companies aren't going to get the sales that they need. But when you are able to try something new, you will find that you can stick out in the minds of your customers and it is easier to sell them the benefits of the product.

Take a look the next time that you are watching television or listen when you are on the radio. Do any of these advertisements or copy speak to you in any way or are they all about the company or all the same as the others? In most cases, you probably won't find that any of them stick out in your mind and once you move on to your song or your show, you will no longer remember them. Is this something that you want to have happen with your copy?

Trying something new can be scary, but it is what will make your copy stand out against all the other companies and products that are available. As long as you have your research to back it up and you can prove that this is going to speak to the customers you want to reach, it is not a bad idea. Your client may even be impressed with the new options because they want to speak out from the crowd, they want to get the attention, so pitch them the idea, perhaps with a few other safe ones if you aren't sure how they are going to respond, and you will find that these big and new ideas are going to be the best received.

The way that you try something new is going to vary between the medium that you use. These new things aren't going to be the same when you are using a billboard as it would for an eBook or for a television ad. But if you think of an idea that you think will stand out, you should give it a try and see where it is going to lead. You may be surprised at the results that you are able to get and the response from the client when they realize that they are going to be able to attract more customers.

Conclusion

Becoming a copywriter can be an exciting experience. You are going to have a lot of luck writing for a variety of customers and making some good money, whether you work for just one client on a full time basis or you are looking to work on a freelance basis. There are quite a few different things that you are able to do within the copywriting business and you will be able to pick from some of the most exciting opportunities that you can think of in between the products, the clients, and more.

This guidebook is going to discuss some of the things that you need to do in order to become a world class copywriter. You don't necessarily need to have the right experience behind you to do this, even those who are just getting started can do well with this career choice if they have the right things in place. This guidebook will talk about the ten things that you need to have in order to get stared with copywriting and see the success that you desire!

CPSIA information can be obtained
at www.ICGtesting.com
Printed in the USA
BVHW031459171022
649633BV00008B/785